HIST in HURRY

Stone Age

written and drawn by
JOHN FARMAN

MACMILLAN
CHILDREN'S BOOKS

All **HISTORY** in a **HURRY** *titles can be ordered at your local bookshop or are available by post from Book Service by Post (tel: 01624 675137).*

First published 1999 by Macmillan Children's Books
a division of Macmillan Publishers Limited
25 Eccleston Place, London SW1W 9NF
Basingstoke and Oxford
www.macmillan.co.uk

Associated companies throughout the world

ISBN 0 330 37648 9

Printed and bound in Great Britain by Mackays of Chatham plc, Kent

☙ CONTENTS

∰ OFF WE GO!

Right up to the early part of the 1800s, everyone (including scientists) believed that man simply arrived on earth one day looking just as he does now (a bit like that nice Mr Adam and Mrs Eve). I suppose all the other creatures, from ants to zebras and aardvarks to . . . er, more zebras,* turned up at the same time, all neat and tidy-like, and ready to go. I don't think so. (By the way, don't you girls get cross with me if I only refer to 'man' throughout this book – it's just too boring to write 'Stone Age man and woman' every time. Sorry!)

Then Charles Darwin, a small naturalist with a big beard, who'd been happily sailing around the world searching for bugs and things on a beagle,** discovered something that was to rock the world of science – not to mention religion. In his book, *Origin of Species by Means of Natural Selection* (published in 1859), he delivered to a gobsmacked world his theory that all the animals and creatures in the world once crawled, hopped or slithered out of one huge primeval soup, then separated into different types and then developed by natural selection. Natural selection means that only the strongest, fastest, cleverest and probably grumpiest ones in each lot survived to turn into the creatures we know to this day.

This, as you might imagine, caused mayhem amongst the pompous Victorians, who, while not being at all concerned about where the minor beasts came from, got it into their thick, outraged skulls that Mr Darwin was implying that the human race (i.e. *them*) had developed *directly* from monkeys.

---

* Couldn't think of anything else beginning with Z, eh? Ed
** The *Beagle* was the name of the ship he sailed on. Ed

Poor Charles was ridiculed throughout the country, as this rhyme in a comic opera of the time, by Gilbert and Sullivan, suggests.

Darwinian Man,
Though well behaved,
At best
Is only a monkey shaved.

Wrong End of the Stick

They had got what he was saying totally wrong. Well, sort of wrong! Darwin had actually stated that, although we humans share loads of ape-like characteristics (see *Gladiators* and *Blind Date*), the primitive being that we (and that includes you) developed from was not quite the same as the one that turned into your average chimp. It's a bit like comparing a typewriter and a computer. Clever as the invention of the typewriter might have been, it could only have developed into a better typewriter; in other words, it had reached the limit of its possibilities. A computer on the other hand, much like the human being, seems to be able to keep on developing (and that's scary).

Nuts to You

Having said that, your ancestors *did* swing about in trees, eat nuts and stuff and make an awful noise when cross. If you've any doubts, feel that little lump at the bottom of your spine. That, I'm afraid, proves that you (well, maybe not you personally) did once have a tail.

It was when man decided to stop swinging about in the branches, come down to earth and get off his hands and knees, and when he discovered the merits of hitting soft things (animals and wood) with hard things (weapons and tools made out of stone) that the period we call the Stone Age, and our story, begins. These are the guys that we're going to take a closer look at.

Officially, the Stone Age began 2,400,000 years ago (on a Tuesday) and lasted . . . until it was over. OK, OK – until they discovered metal (around 6500 BC).

By the way, please ignore those niggly little comments at the bottom of the page (signed *Ed*). That's just my editor, Susie, having a go at me.

Chapter 1

MR AND MRS PREHISTORIC MAN (AND THE ROTTEN RISS)

Although it seems rather obvious, the word 'prehistoric' means 'before history', which really means 'before anyone had a clue how to write anything down'. Therefore, everything we know about our ancient relatives has had to come from what has been found by scrapers and diggers and the people who interpreted what the scrapers and diggers . . . um, scraped and digged.*

So, when did Stone Age man first appear? It seems that *Homo erectus* (the first man to stand on his own two feet) was around well before (a million years well before) the first *Homo sapiens* (meaning bright and intelligent – like what we are). We,

WHAT DOES BRIGHT AND INTELLIGENT MEAN?

* Dug! Ed

in fact, were around from 300,000 years ago – give or take a month.

Where to Live?
About 250,000 years ago, there were around 10,000,000 humans (about the population of Tokyo today) on our planet. They tended to live in the places with nice weather – Europe, China, Clacton-on-Sea and Africa – avoiding the too hot deserts and the too cold icy places. This is somewhat understandable when you realize that they didn't have anoraks, trousers, socks, thermal vests, air conditioning or central heating!

Europe 250,000 years ago was best of all. For a start, it was much warmer than it is now, with animals like water buffalo and monkeys swinging in the trees.* And there sure were a lot of trees for them to swing in. Most of the continent was beautiful woodland with patches of lush meadow in between, and rivers running in between them. Down in the Mediterranean areas (where the monkeys swung) were steamy rainforests.

Cold Snap
For Stone Age man, avoiding the cold had always been a bit of a problem, but this became especially tricky 200,000 years ago when a terrible Ice Age called the 'Riss' came along. Luckily it only lasted a mere 75,000 years which, although extremely irritating if your lifespan actually fell within it, was, in history terms, a mere blink.

Ice Ages are simply no fun. Just as we today are experiencing global warming, the early *Homo sapiens* of

* Buffalo swinging in the trees? Ed

200,000 years ago noticed their barometers beginning to plummet*. At first the trees began to wither, especially in the Mediterranean areas (along with the monkeys, I presume), and then the first flakes of snow fell on the mountains. And, oh boy, did it snow. Gradually, especially in Europe, the snow filled up the bits between the mountains and as it got deeper and deeper, the stuff at the bottom became squeezed into thick (mile-thick!) ice. Now, thick ice tends to be heavy and slippery – and because of both of these things it began to slide, scraping off all the topsoil, grass and grazing animals everywhere it went – right down to naked rock. The sea then began to fill up with icebergs and the poor people (and all the animals that were around at the time) found themselves caught between massive impassable sheets of ice (which covered a third of the world), trapped on the last remaining bits of scrubby land.

In Africa and the deserts of Asia, the previously hot, sweaty Stone-Agers were getting the cooler weather and lush vegetation that Europe had enjoyed before; trees and shrubs grew where there had been desert, and open woodlands flourished where there had been drippy rainforests. So the poor people in the colder bits, like Europe, guessing that there might be better weather elsewhere, packed their bags (or would have done if they'd had any) and began moving across towards Africa and Asia in droves.

Back home in Britain, however, it was as cold as the shady side of a witch's cat (is that right?). So much so that, even in high summer, if the average cave family had decided to go off to the seaside for their hols, they'd have had to pack their sledges and snowshoes. Not only that, but they'd've had to walk a lot further to find the blinking sea, because water levels

* They didn't have barometers. Ed

had dropped by as much as 150 metres as the sea turned into ice. So much, in fact, that you could *stroll* over to France (except it wasn't called that) for the day.

Useless Fact No. 980

Did you know that there was a mini-Ice Age that started in the 16th century and ended around 1750? This kicked off the obsession with fur on human clothing that has lasted more than two centuries.

The World Outside the Cave

So there you are, a nice new caveman, lounging in your cave entrance. What would you have seen from under that thick ridge of bone that ran over your early eyes? Quite a lot! Across the vast, freezing open plains would be loads of delicious animals as far as the eye could see. Little ones like rabbits and rats, middle-sized ones like horses, goats and reindeer, and great big ones like rhinos, buffalo and elephants. Not forgetting all the nasty savage beasts that were out to eat *them* – wolves, lions, tigers, panthers, hamsters,* etc.

Fire Time

The good thing about having a bad time, however, is that it makes a chap think harder in order to survive (try being a writer!), and early man was no exception. It is thought (by those who think) that human intelligence grew considerably during the 75,000-year Riss period. As for the animals, loads of species disappeared, but the stronger ones, like the rhino and the elephant, simply grew thick woolly coats to keep themselves warm. It is also thought that it was during the Riss Ice Age that old *Homo sapiens* finally got the idea of fire and proper warm clothes.

Photofit

But what did these first proper *Homo sapiens* look like? Well, although being a bit monkey-like (receding forehead, deep-set eyes, sticky-out jaw, etc.) in the face department, they probably had quite 'modern' bodies – the average height of a man then being 1.68 metres. (It's about 10 cm more today.) They had brains that were bigger than their ancestors' (*Homo erectus*) and nearly as big as ours.** They would have been quite rugged in build but at the same time jolly athletic – they'd've had to be, to have any chance of catching their supper (and to avoid being

* Have you gone mad? Ed
** Not difficult in your case, Mr Farman. Ed

supper for something else). Crikey, these days all we have to do is walk from the bus stop or car park to the supermarket – no wonder we're turning into a race of fat slobs!

HOMO BLOBBO

Useless Fact No. 982
The way our lazy human race is going (or not going), our legs will soon drop off through lack of use. That's natural selection for you, Mr Darwin!

Chapter 2

WARM-UP TIME

The dreaded Riss Ice Age ended around 125,000 years ago, as the temperature began to rise. The glaciers melted like ice cubes in a glass of warm Coke and the sea came right up to the cavemen's knees again. Suddenly Europe reopened for business and the more ambitious Stone-Agers began to drift back. Man had developed into what we now call *Neanderthal*, the first fully developed, proper-brained (size-wise) human being. He still looked a bit primitive, admittedly – but not much more than some people you see at footy matches on a Saturday afternoon.*

* You simply can't say things like that. Ed
I just did. JF

Useless Question No. 1
If having as large a brain as possible is reckoned to be a Good Thing, why did ours stop getting bigger 100,000 years ago?

How Do We Know?
It all started one day in 1856 in the Neanderthal (Neander Valley), near Düsseldorf in Germany, when a very old man (or should I say the skeleton of a very old man) was dug up. Actually that's not true. He hadn't been that old when he died, but he had been dead for rather a long time (30,000 years to be not very precise). So, in fact, although the skeleton was old . . . well, you get the point. He was, by this time, a fossil – the first fossil of a man ever to be found (apart from my old history teacher).

Useless Fact No. 986
The Neander Valley was named after a local celebrity called Joachim Neumann which means 'new man' (the Greek for new man is *neander*) – odd coincidence, eh!

Unfortunately Darwin's *Origin of Species* hadn't been published yet, so no one believed that the old man could be nearly as old as he was, cos that would make him older than Adam. And that would mean rewriting the Old Testament and rethinking the whole of the Christian religion (and the Jewish, and the Islamic) – which would never do.

Because the original Neanderthal man had a bent, almost deformed body, the big palaeontologists (studiers of fossils) of the day made him out to be a shambling monster, a bit like Frankenstein's lad. Many held the view that the poor chap was a completely different species to modern man and represented the final dead end in his own evolutionary story.

Not So!

It all changed in the 1950s when more leading palaeontologists had another look at our hero and concluded that he was merely a crippled specimen of a far finer sort of bloke. This meant that despite *his* desperate stoop, there was no reason why his mates shouldn't have been as fine and upright as you or I.*

In fact, the image of the stumbling, hands-touching-ground, gorilla-like caveman had to be completely reconsidered, especially when graves were found containing remains similar to the Neanderthal man and, amazingly, all the paraphernalia of proper man-made burials – stones, flowers, hymn books and all. (Well, maybe not hymn books.) These guys might not have qualified as male models looks-wise (thank goodness), but the emerging evidence of the way they lived lifted them much higher on that old evolutionary ladder.

* Who are you kidding? Ed

Gradually reports began to emerge of primitive stone tools dating back to the same period being found in caves near the burial sites. The proper study of Stone Age man was about to begin.

Chapter 3

TOOL TIME

Making a tool or implement out a bit of old flint may not seem a big deal to you, but imagine if you'd never even heard of a tool before, let alone seen one. In the brilliant sci-fi movie *2001: A Space Odyssey*, the action starts with angry apes bashing things (and then each other) with bits of wood and bone. This symbolized the start of civilization. But while the monkeys just continued bashing themselves with anything they could lay their hands on, man was the first to try to *adapt* these things into 'tools' to do specific jobs.

Useless Fact No. 988
A pointed length of wood was dug up at the seaside resort of Clacton-on-Sea, Essex. The handle off some kid's bucket and spade? Oh no, it turned out to be one of the oldest spears ever found. It was carbon-dated at 300,000 years.

UseFUL Fact No. 1
Carbon dating is the ultra-amazing process that today's scientists use to find out how old things are. They check the nitrogen content of an organic thing in proportion to the loss of carbon. Apparently, carbon decays at a constant rate.

The jobs that Stone Age man's tools had to do were not that subtle. They needed:

Flat, choppy-type things to cut wood for the fire.

⟫ Sharp, pointy-type things to throw at animals and stab them.

⟫ Sharp, daggery-type things to cut the meat into bits.

⟫ Flat, scrapy-type things to get the flesh off the animals' skins to make clothing and primitive tents.

Flint Stones

The best kind of stone for the job was flint as, when struck hard, it splinters or flakes and, if hit enough times, eventually ends up with a fine edge. The first Neanderthal tools were pretty crude, and it's often hard to tell whether some bits of stone we've discovered really were man-made or not – but towards the end of their period they got really good at flaking the flint, and produced some fine specialized tools and weapons.

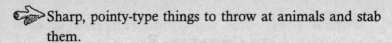

It's interesting to note that the idea of eating the flesh of one's fellow beast was down to Neanderthal man's fourbears.* (The great apes, unlike *Homo erectus*, did – and still do – live almost exclusively on salads.) But animals didn't just come round to the front door of the cave and demand to be eaten – you had to chase 'em.

* I think you mean forebears. Ed

Whereas *Homo erectus* simply had sharpened sticks as hunting weapons, Neanderthal man learned to tip his spears with sharpened stones. He would also use the splintered bones of animals, which is a bit weird when you come to think of it: using a bone off one animal to murder another. But I doubt whether Stone Age man gave a fig about that. He was hungry!

There's been a lot of evidence discovered to show that there were all sorts of primitive weapon 'factories' in ancient times, producing these flint tools. One cave in the Lebanon was thought to have been occupied for 50,000 years and over a million man-sharpened flints were uncovered. It's difficult to know when man first got the idea of joining the flints to wooden handles but, for the early period at least, Neanderthal man stuck to just holding his weapons in his hand, with maybe a bit of animal hide to protect him from the sharp edges.

Stone Balls

There is also pretty good evidence that they carved heavy, hand-sized stone balls, to which they tied long strips of hide to make what became known as *bolas.* They'd whirl these around their heads and fling them at the doomed animals' legs in order to trip the poor beggars up.

Useless Fact No. 990

One of Stone Age man's favourite tricks was to round up a bunch of animals, chase them up to and over the edge of a cliff, and then pick 'em up at the bottom – dead! Smart thinking!

Best Tools

Having had such a hard time during the Riss period, European cavemen had to be pretty innovative in their tool-making, and they promptly invented the double-edged axe, chiselled on both sides to achieve extra sharpness. They then realized that if you started with an oval or round stone and bashed away at it, what was left would be the ultra-sharp core and that the rounded edge of that then cut much better. Not only that, but the flakes they knocked off made perfect little tools in themselves – so nothing was wasted.

Cold Again

They became so good at weapon-making, hunting and hence warm clothing ('borrowed off' animals), that when the next Ice Age (called the Würm) arrived, around 75,000 years ago, many no longer felt the need to pack up and go searching for sunnier climes. Neanderthal man lived off the massive herds of reindeer, woolly rhinos and mammoths that continually trekked through his backyard (Europe).

Useless Fact No. 992

As the various ice ages came and went, so did the bodily hair on Stone Age man and woman. Clever, eh!

Useless Fact No. 993

You will notice that I only talk about them eating meat. This is because, unfortunately, they didn't eat their greens. This was because the landscape was largely tundra – moss, etc. Great for animals but no good for us lot. In other words, there weren't any vegetables to speak of.

Travelling in Prehistoric Times

Usually when one sets out on a long journey, one has a fair idea of where one is going. When Neanderthal man set out, he hadn't a clue – and why should he? There were no papers, maps, holiday brochures or travel programmes on the TV, so when he left the comfort of his own cave with his wife and kids, his only thought was to get away from the biting cold. They must have looked wistfully at the distant mountains, without a clue as to what was on the other side.

FIRST MAP

Stone Age man and his family travelled on foot with no luggage and no surplus food. If they wanted to eat they had to catch it (there were no shops). Their progress was slow – but in a way it didn't matter. Let's face it, these days if we set off round the world in a plane, we can reach most places in a matter of hours. In those ancient days, the travelling could take years – whole generations slowly on the move. Sometimes they might drift for hundreds of years, stopping for a while if they liked a place, and then moving on if it got colder. If they caught diseases and plagues, which they often did, they'd stop for considerably longer (like for ever). The population of the world was, therefore, continually on the move – or not (on account of being dead).

Chapter 4

⤳ BURNING BRIGHT

To say we take fire for granted these days is no exaggeration. Most homes have several sources of switch-on flame – whether it be matches, lighters, the cooker or the gas fire. Even your car (or your mum or dad's car) works on a series of little fires or explosions in the combustion . . . er, engine bit. For thousands of years, fire has been at the centre of all life. Without it we wouldn't be able to cook, keep warm, manufacture things, or even have barbecues.

Got a Light?
Imagine, therefore, a time when man didn't know how to make it! He'd probably witnessed it – natural fires from volcanoes and lightning would happen every now and again and no doubt would scare the living daylights out of him. Imagine how frightening fire must have been if you had no idea what it was!

IGNORANCE IS BLISS →

This is probably why fire in ancient times was always connected with magic, superstition or any of the other mumbo-jumbo that people who don't know much better get into.

Before Stone Age men found out how to make fire themselves, it is believed that they lit sticks from the embers of volcanoes (dodgy or what?) and natural fires and tried to keep them alight as long as possible. If their personal fire went out, they could probably go round to a neighbour's and take a light off theirs – and vice versa. Some historians even believe that they would have fought over fire if necessary. This way of doing things, so the experts say, went on for thousands of years until, presumably, one day some clever-Stone-Age-clogs learned how to do it himself.

DIY Fire

I'd love to be able to tell you who the first person was to make a fire – you know, someone called Ug or Zog or something – but as Stone Age man was a bit behind in the old writing-things-down-for-future-generations department, we'll never know. What we *can* be pretty sure of is that whoever he (or she) was, they could have had no idea of what they'd started. The thinking goes that whoever lit the first fire was probably fiddling around sharpening a flint axehead and noticed little sparks flying from the impact of his stone. This must have happened a trillion times before one of these sparks made anything catch fire. The likelihood was that this particular pioneer, on the big day, had been using a piece of iron pyrite as his hammering stone, which would have caused the heat from the spark to last just long enough to light something (like his hair). Sparks from iron, so I'm told, develop additional heat through combustion in the air.

Quite a bit later on, fire making became less haphazard, when they discovered friction – either rubbing bits of wood together, or making a sort of drill (fire drill?) – that is, twirling a stick around in a hole till it gets hot. This method of creating fire might well have been discovered by some bright spark* who noticed the heat created by the friction when branches of trees rubbed together in a strong wind. Well, it *might*!

I THINK THAT'S THE ENERGY ASSOCIATED WITH THE RANDOM MOTION OF THE MOLECULES, ATOMS OR SMALLER STRUCTURAL UNITS OF WHICH MATTER IS COMPOSED

What's Cooking?

Let's leap ahead to the time when our intrepid Stone-Ager had a nice little fire burning in his cave. There was plenty of wood

* Is that your idea of a joke? *Ed*

around to keep it going – and even coal if he could be bothered to dig for it. Early man was probably just as careless as we are, and it is pretty obvious that his fires must occasionally have got out of hand, creating massive grassland and forest infernos. We can suppose that when the fire had burned out, he must have come across the charred bodies of some of the animals that hadn't run fast enough. We can also suppose that they must have smelled and tasted much, much better (having been freshly roasted). It doesn't take a great modern mind to realize that this was probably how he first discovered the joys of cooked animals (sorry, if you're a veggie!).

Useless Fact No. 995

Very early, early man (Homo erectus) had developed huge, powerful jaws for tearing and chewing the tough raw meat. It is reasonable to suppose that when Neanderthal man discovered cooking and therefore tenderizing his supper, he no longer needed such a big, strong mouth. Natural selection (see page 4), presumably, then took over and small jaws became all the rage.

Staying Put

Being able to create a fire and sit round it removed the need to search for warmer places to live when the chilly spells came along. Most families or communities, therefore, tended to hang around one area from then on. When you have fire in your cave you must have a place for it called – you've guessed – a *fireplace*. Once you've got a fireplace, small friendly animals like dogs and cats* will generally creep up to lie in front of it. Fires also give off light and this meant that Mr Neanderthal's bedtime could be when he wanted, and not when the sun went down.

* Cats weren't domesticated until Egyptian times – only a few thousand years BC. Ed
Whoops! JF

With this new light in his cave, he probably looked round the walls and found them a bit bare. I know, he thought, we'll have a few animal pictures – which he then proceeded to do – thus creating the first cave paintings (see Chapter 6).

So there he is, lounging round the fire after a mammoth steak supper (literally), with his wives (or should I say partners) beside him making clothes, the kids playing a very early version of Monopoly (before Park Lane and Mayfair) in the firelight, and the family pets snoozing by the embers. A cosy domestic scene, eh! Before he knew it, *Homo sapiens* had created what came to be known as the first HOME (*Homo home?*).

Chapter 5

JUST AN
AVERAGE
STONE AGE DAY

The scene is a darkened cave somewhere near Greater London (or where Greater London would have been had it existed).

It's 7.30, Tuesday morning, 3 November,* and the year is 58,764 BC. Actually, I lied about that: times, dates, hours and years were only recorded relatively recently – but you get the picture.

Anyway, Mr Neanderthal, cold and grumpy, rubs his eyes, crawls out from under his woolly rhino (skin), and stumbles over to kick the fire that appears to have gone out. He curses

some ancient Stone Age curse and trudges across the dark, stinking cave (no lavs or bathrooms in those days) towards the cave entrance. A hide curtain has been put up overnight to keep out the cold and to hide the family from wild animals.

Useless Fact No. 997

One of the most dangerous of these animals was the cave bear. These massive chaps weighed up to 700 kilograms, could grow to 2.5 metres in height and were always jumping out on you when you weren't looking. There were once so many of the darned things that in some places literally tons of their bones were found and ground up for fertilizer. What a fate!

Meanwhile . . . back at the cave

Mr Neanderthal peers out and curses again. The ground is covered with a thick layer of snow. Ice Ages really were boring on a daily basis. Having said that, early man could live in much colder climates than we can now (we're just a bunch of softies). If you consider that pigs, who have skins not much thicker than ours, walk around stark naked in the coldest weather, you realize that man, who is, after all, just a medium-sized animal (and a bit of a pig at times), may once have been the same. It's all a question of what you're used to. My grandparents lived in a freezing house with no central heating and—*

Sorry . . . where was I ? Ah yes, luckily Mr Neanderthal had brought a whole load of twigs and branches into the cave last night, so he gets his fire-making tools out and starts the long process of trying to light some dried-out bracken before chucking the twigs and branches on. When the fire is crackling

* Can we get back to the Stone-Agers, please? Ed

and the cave starts to warm up, the kids begin to stir. At first they think they're late for school, but then they remember, just in time, that it hasn't been invented yet.

Useless and Not Very Nice Fact No. 999

Most of the children in Stone Age times would be boys – not by coincidence, but because in so many primitive societies (and even China now) boys were regarded as being much better than girls. Boys were best because they would turn out to be hunters, and a primitive group could only support a certain amount of non-hunters. What happened to the baby girls? Nobody really knows, but I dare say you could guess.

WHAT A LOVELY GIRL

Meanwhile . . . Breakfast

One of our hero's women (they always had a few spares) goes to the fire and pushes away the embers to reveal a few flat stones, glowing red-hot by now. Another one goes to the underground meat pit outside (even they understood about keeping their meat cold) and brings back a couple of hunks of venison (dead deer) that Dad killed a couple of days ago. Dad likes his meat rather on the rare side, so after the lump has been on the griddle for only a couple of minutes, he whips it off with his bare hands and starts tearing at it with his big, strong, pointy teeth in a most uncouth manner. In fact, Mr Neanderthal's table manners generally leave a lot to be desired, but that's not surprising, because he hasn't even got a table – let alone a plate . . . or a knife . . . or a fork. The kids, who are now out of bed, scrabble in the dirt for the gristly bits that he throws aside. Their breakfast will come later, when Dad goes hunting with his mates.

Talking or Not

There seems little doubt that the one thing that separated man from monkey was man's ability to talk to his mates. Unfortunately, because he never wrote anything down, we don't have a clue as to how he spoke or how many words he used. We also don't know whether every single group or society had its own personal language. It seems pretty reasonable to think that, as there were no books, there was no way that a language could spread very far. Having no books also meant that the poor devils couldn't learn about anything outside their own immediate experiences. In other words early man remained totally in the dark, education-wise, for thousands of years, and his progress out of it was p-a-i-n-f-u-l-l-y s-l-o-w.

Meanwhile . . . a knock at the door

Well, there would have been – if they'd had a door. Outside are the other guys from the colony, weapons in hand, ready for the day's hunt. Dad puts on an extra skin and, after a couple of greeting grunts, disappears with the lads into the snowy wastes.

Coco Pops? No Way!

Now the nippers can have *their* breakfast – a kind of Stone-Age muesli, made up of nuts, berries, seeds and all the stuff that they'd gathered in the woods. Every morning the kids dream of something like hot chocolate, but their mothers insist they drink the cold ex-snow since that's all they've got. Although the Neanderthals seemed to have got the hang of killing things, they hadn't got the hang of milking things yet. Mind you, would you want to milk a woolly rhino?

NOT INVENTED
YET

Mad Hutters

Oddly enough, not all cavemen lived in caves, because, quite simply, there were loads of places that didn't have any. There's a lot of evidence from 'those what dig' (archaeologists) that primitive man knew how to build primitive huts. They were rather flimsy, however, made out of bent twigs and thatched with grass, leaves or bracken. Having not yet thought of holes in roofs as chimneys, the fire would be placed near the entrance so that the smoke could escape. If it had been down to me, I'd have put it up the other end so that *I* could escape if and when the blasted hut caught fire.

Chapter 6

ART IN THE DARK

One of the great problems with painting pictures in caves is that you can't see what you're doing. As I said before, early man could do little, artwise, indoors until fire was invented. Even then it was not ideal. For a start, fire has a nasty habit of flickering – especially in a draught – so whatever our poor budding artist was painting must have wobbled like mad.

Useless Fact No. 1001

In the awe-inspiring and perfectly preserved prehistoric caves at Lascaux (South of France), amongst little clay figurines and ivory carvings, were found lots of crude oil lamps made out of mud, shells and even the skulls of animals (spooky!). They used the fat from melted-down animals as fuel with just a bit of fibre to act as a wick.

Basically, it appears that Neanderthal man hardly got beyond not very good scratches on the wall. Proper cave art was to follow later on in the Stone Age.

Most artists these days have nice bright, warm studios to do their 'thing' in, but the poor old cavepersons not only had to put up with semi-darkness, but severe dampness and crippling cold. Worse still, they ran the risk of being buried under tons of rock or jumped on by nasty things that lurked in dark corners (see Chapter 10). The very earliest images were a bit like graffiti – the sort of stuff you see in bus shelters, scratched into the rock by bits of sharp flint. Later they found out how to make paint, by pounding down coloured rocks and then mixing the powder with fat, blood and sometimes even urine.

How They Did It

First of all the painter would scratch the outline of whatever he was going to have a go at with his trusty flint. If it was an animal (and it usually was) he'd have to remember what it looked like as best he could – I mean, he couldn't take the animal's photo or ask it to come in and pose, could he? And he certainly couldn't take the wall outside.

Useless Fact No. 1004

Many learned historians believe that some of the cavemen might have had the amazing and these days seldom heard of ability to project the image of some remembered object (using only their minds) on to a blank bit of wall and simply draw round it. Sounds a bit of a cheat to me . . .

Nothing to Copy

However he did it, Stone Age man was certainly breaking new ground: unlike us, he could hardly ever have seen a painting before so he'd have no styles or shortcuts to copy or rip off. He'd have known nothing about perspective (things getting smaller as they get further away) and would have had no idea that you could show depth by shading. He therefore drew everything sideways on, just like little kids (or old Egyptians) do (or did), with no interest in backgrounds. In order to show movement, he would always draw the animals' legs in the stretched position as if running.

Meanwhile, back at the cave wall . . .

Having finished all the line work, the main parts of the picture were filled in with colour, using either tied-up bundles of animal hair or sticks with the ends crushed or chewed – or by blowing paint through reed or bone pipes. I don't know about you, but I wouldn't have got much of a buzz out of blowing paint made of pee through a tube, even if it did look nice.

3-D

Early Stone Age sculpture was not nearly as good – probably because their tools were so crude – but they did do some rather cute little engravings of animals on bones.

What For?

These days, paintings are usually done to create something pleasing to look at, make the artist a few quid or cover a damp patch on the wall. Cave paintings, on the other hand, were apparently done for a whole load of other reasons. For a start, unlike hunters these days, man had much more of a bond with the animals that he chased, killed and eventually ate. Because he was so much closer to being an animal himself, this relationship was a strange mixture of mystical, religious and magical impulses. To stand any chance of catching his prey he had to study them day in and day out, to the point that he knew their ways as well as the poor things did themselves. I'm sure the hunter guys even dreamed of the animals at night.

However, I doubt that the beasts cared much either way – they still ended up being eaten!

Drawing People

Although Stone Age man later became rather a whizz at painting animals, he never quite got the hang of people. There seems to be no real reason for this, as, if anything, you'd have thought it would have been easier to draw something that would sit still in front of him, rather than something that was always running about. In the big wall paintings men were only represented in stick form. Women were often better drawn, though usually represented when pregnant. This is because pregnancy in both animals and humans was regarded with great respect – even awe. In animals it meant more food and in people it meant . . . more people.

Despite there being very few drawings of women in the later Stone Age, there were quite a lot of sculptures, mostly little and mostly carved out of bone, ivory or stone. Their heads are often peculiarly like those of the animals their menfolk hunted, but there is a theory (a bit far-fetched, if you ask me) that they might have worn masks when having their sculptures done. It's more likely that the sculptures didn't represent any woman in particular, just woman in general – as symbols of fertility and replenishment.

Hands Up

The current theory for the lack of pictures of humans is that early man might have thought that people were inferior to animals and therefore not worth getting their paints out for. Having said that, it's a well-known fact that among primitive people, drawing a likeness of your enemy gains great control over him. Maybe that goes for animals too!

The most spooky evidence of the existence of early man was his love of leaving handprints, either dipped in paint and pressed on the wall, or as a silhouette. The latter would have been done by placing a hand on the wall and blowing paint at it through a pipe.

Useless Fact No. 1007

It's interesting to note that many of the handprints show fingers missing. Historians believe that finger removal (even from kids) was all the rage in those days as a sort of religious/magical ritual. Finger removal featured big in the ceremonies of North American Indians, Aborigines, Tongans, and Fijians.

Rave in a Cave?

Stone Age man *might* have been a great singer and dancer, but there's no way we'll ever know. The likelihood is, however, that the sort of music he made would be similar to that of the Aborigines today.

Come to that, he *might* have been a whole load of things, but we'll never know, so does it really matter?

Chapter 7

NEARLY PERFECT (UPPER PALAEOLITHIC TIMES)

Evolution-wise, Stone Age man had just about reached the end of his long path, which sadly meant he was as good as he was gonna get. About 35,000 years ago, the period we call Upper Palaeolithic began and Cro-Magnon man (the first proper recognizable *Homo sapiens*) appeared in Europe.

Useless Fact No. 1010
The first chap to get the name Cro-Magnon was actually a skeleton found in a cave in a hill of the same name in France.

Mr Cro-Magnon was no doubt descended from the gang that had almost certainly walked across from the Middle East or Africa as soon as all those nasty Ice Ages finished. Unlike the Neanderthals, who all looked much the same, this lot were mongrels – combinations of all sorts. They lived a much more sophisticated life than the people they replaced, existing in smallish groups of 50 to 60. They met up with other groups on special occasions and it was then that all the matchmaking took place, essential if they were to avoid chronic inbreeding and severe nuttiness. However, it is difficult to know what they were really like as all we have to go on are their paintings and a few old bones.

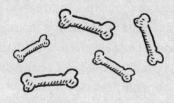

New for Old?

The old theory that Neanderthal man was gradually forced out by the new boys is now discredited and proper palaeontologists now prefer the theory that Neanderthal man gradually *became* Cro-Magnon man, through inter-'marriage' (for want of a better word!). Either way, poor old Mr Neanderthal, who'd never really got the hang of talking (on account of his underdeveloped voicebox), would have been at a terrible disadvantage amongst the chatty newcomers.

How do we know all this? Well, in 1868, in the Dordogne area of the south of France, a load of ancient bones were found in five archaeological layers. The newest of the bones (on the top), dated at between 10,000 and 35,000 years old, were a slightly improved model of the old Neanderthal chappie. Cro-Magnon man was powerfully built, well-muscled, about 1.70 metres tall with a short wide face, small teeth and a long skull – just as well cos it housed a brain that was slightly larger than yours or mine.*

To the outward observer (if he could have hung around for

* Let's just say yours, shall we? Ed
OK, yours. JF

50,000 years) the heavy Neanderthal ridge over the eyes gradually disappeared, and the brow went upwards, instead of straight back like a monkey's. Most noticeable of all, the huge chinless jaw (again, like a monkey's) disappeared, along with the bulge at the back of the skull (thought to have developed as a balance to his massive mouth). Cro-Magnon man was, by all accounts, becoming quite a looker. It is said that if you'd dressed him in modern clothes, given him a haircut and let him loose in the street, nobody would notice the difference (unless they asked him the time, of course).

Useless Fact No. 1013

If you want to see the nearest we get to a real live Cro-Magnon man, still walking about today, take a holiday in the Canary Islands. Apparently, the native Guanchos still retain most of their features.

Useless Fact No. 1015

All the Neanderthal men that were ever found were almost the same. This seems to prove the point that the poor bloke had reached the end of his path – evolution-wise. It wasn't his fault, but it must be said that he'd had simply ages to reach a modern appearance if he was ever going to.

Good Tools

The most instantly recognizable thing about Cro-Magnon man is that he developed far more sophisticated tools for his everyday life. The main differences were as follows:

The cutting tools he produced were twice as long as they were wide and could now be referred to as blades. The advantage was that he could produce more cutting edge per kilogram of stone.

The blades were much more finely made, and sometimes so narrow that they resembled chisels (called *burins*).

The Périgordian period (South of France) featured tools thought to have originated in south-west Asia. These were long curved knives sharpened on both sides.

Other Big Cro-Magnon Firsts

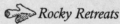*Rocky Retreats*

Cro-Magnon man distinguished himself when he found out how to make primitive huts out of rocks, either up against overhanging cliffs or free-standing. He and his mates lived in these all year round, only moving on when the animals ran out (or ran away).

At the Jeweller's

He was the first to produce any recognizable form of jewellery. Hunters would drill holes into the teeth of their prey (early dentistry?) and hang them round their necks. There have also been pieces of polished and painted ivory found that were almost certain to have been used as bodily decoration.

 What's the Date?

The only explanation for the bones found with equal groups of scratches on them, is that Cro-Magnon man was trying his level best to invent some kind of calendar, to work out what day it was.

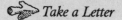 *Take a Letter*

From marks made in paintings or on bones, it is thought that Cro-Magnon man was the first person in the world ever to think up a system of writing. Trouble was, he couldn't read, so it probably wasn't much use.*

* That's the silliest joke in the book. Ed

Chapter 8

AT HOME WITH HOMO SAPIENS

Gradually modern man (*Homo sapiens*) split into three major racial groups – Caucasoids in Europe, Mongoloids in Asia, and Negroids in Africa. In Australia a minor group (the Australoids) were to become the Aborigines. These early groups or tribes were the first to have a structure to their society.

Running the show would be the chieftain and the *shaman*. The chieftain's role is fairly obvious: he had to be the strongest, the top hunter and the protector of his gang. But the real power lay with the shaman (a sort of witch doctor): not only did he deal with medicine and magic, but he was also the go-between between the tribe and the spirits of the dead (primitive people had a big thing about their lost relatives). The shaman specialized in curses and spells and to the ordinary man-in-the-cave he could either cure you or curse you, depending on how he felt. The shaman should be regarded as the first real intellectual – a dealer in dreams and art. His henchmen would be all the artists, dancers, singers, storytellers and TV personalities (Mystic Meg?).

Sculpture for All

As well as painting the paintings that adorned his walls, man was becoming more and more interested in sculpture. The most popular subject was the female form, which he portrayed with hugely exaggerated breasts, bellies and buttocks (unless they really *were* like that!!). The theory is that these figures, like the drawings mentioned in Chapter 6, did not represent any woman in particular but were fertility figures to be worshipped and adored – a bit like the producer of all life – Mother Earth – and all that malarkey!

Nice Work

Life as a caveman in those days was probably quite nice, especially if the weather was OK. On sunny days they would sit around outside their caves or rock shelters, preparing food, making tools or getting ready to go out hunting. The kids didn't have to wash or clean their teeth and, although they must have ponged a bit, it didn't matter – everybody did. The only drawback with being dirty was that the slightest cut or graze could turn nasty, and because of this and the millions of diseases that were around, life expectancy was pretty low. Although we know that the shaman and even the old women must have dealt in herbal cures, we have no idea of how effective they were.

Party Time in Caveland

It is also fairly certain that every now and again they would have big celebrations when they would invite nearby tribes over to party. These neighbours would also be required to admire the paintings. In this way certain styles eventually began to spread.

Useless Fact No. 1017

The cave art discovered in Spain and France is older than any other art in the world. All that Chinese, Mesopotamian and Greek stuff is practically brand new in comparison.

Secret Weapons

The tools for spearing animals were becoming even more sophisticated. Some clever clogs worked out that by carving a barb on the end of a spear, it wouldn't fall out of the prey when it ran off. The same went for fishing, and the barbed fishing spears were connected to lines, so that the fish could be pulled out of the water before getting away. This was the beginning of the most popular sport in Britain today. The bow and arrow, which was all the rage over in Africa, didn't hit Europe till much later.

They were getting rather clever with bones as well. The large flat ones could be used as shovels and digging implements, while the small ones were made into primitive buttons and – a great breakthrough – needles for sewing clothes and animal-hide shelters. Antlers were also used in the making of tools and waved about by silly shamans (shamen?) at spiritual gatherings.

In areas where there wasn't much wood the resourceful *Homo sapiens* used the massive mammoth bones, covered by hides, to make their shelters.

Here Come the Trees

It's all very well having an end to your Ice Age, but the *what happens afterwards* is not always for the best. The resulting spread of dense forest greatly reduced the amount of open land where animals could live. Soon, all that was left were little grazing areas in amongst the woodland. Fairly disastrous for the hunters because, as you can imagine, hunting is much more difficult in the woods (cos the animals keep hiding behind trees).

At last the bow and arrow came over from Africa (not before time!), and quickly became essential kit for hunting in the woods. Now the hunter could hide behind the trees and wait for his prey to come to him.

What Next?

The world's population was beginning to grow rapidly, thanks to better weapons, warmer clothes and more successful food hunting. But sooner or later the food supply was going to become a problem – as the more people there are, the more food is needed.* That was, until some bright spark noticed that if he threw seeds on the ground, they would grow into replicas of the plants they'd just come from. He had accidentally discovered . . .

* You amaze me. Ed

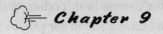# Chapter 9

FARMING
(OR AGRICULTURE,
IF YOU PREFER)

The discovery that seeds were really baby plants that could be collected, stored and then planted in the earth to produce more of the same, came to pass in what we now call the Neolithic (or New Stone Age) Period. The invention of agriculture, the tending and replenishing of animals, the sewing of clothes and the ability to turn mud into bowls and other useful stuff were to follow.

Useless Fact No. 1019

The term Neolithic actually refers to a new type of tool. Basically, man has learned that by grinding and polishing stone to make a sharp edge, instead of all that chipping and flaking, he would have far more control over the finished object. Not only that, but they looked much nicer and impressed his mates. But polished and refined tools were one thing. What to do with them was another.

Agriculture, as we know it, began in Asia Minor around 10,000 years ago, where the long growing seasons, brought on by the increased warmth and plentiful rain, allowed crops to grow and ripen. But the first crops were not necessarily for food. It was more likely that they were grown for fibre, fencing, medicines and even for dyeing hair, bodies or clothing. Early man certainly wouldn't have gone in for proper fields, because these didn't come along until local populations were big enough to need such large amounts of grub. (There was also no point in growing any more than they needed as there was no one to sell the extra to.) The first crops weren't grown to ward off starvation either – far from it. Early *Hungry sapiens* wouldn't have had the time or the patience to watch things grow. He wanted his food right away – or else! The early plantings, therefore, were more like an enjoyable hobby for people who weren't doing too badly anyway, thank you very much (a bit like allotments).

SO WHEN CAN WE EAT IT?

Crops like barley, wheat and lentils came from the Middle East, while rice was first grown in south-east Asia. Not that these were anything like the refined stuff we have these days – crops that have been painstakingly developed over the years. They'd have been very weedy (literally) by comparison.

Animal Crackers

The first animals in the world to be domesticated by man were sheep and goats. (In Europe dogs came first, but obviously couldn't have been sheep dogs because there weren't any sheep yet. I suppose—*)

It was at this time that they realized that by squeezing said sheep in rather personal places, they could get milk, and if that milk was stirred long enough it would turn into cream and then cheese. Best of all, when they got fed up with a particular sheep, they could eat it and wear its clothes. At first they only wore the skins, since clever stuff like cutting off the wool, spinning it, and weaving it into cloth, hadn't been invented yet.

In the colder areas the first animals to be domesticated were reindeer, especially by the nomadic tribes (and maybe a certain Mr F. Christmas) who quite liked taking their dinner and their potential clothing with them wherever they went.

Useless Fact No. 1020

It is thought that prehistoric man might have invented the modern trick of castrating (look it up) all male domesticated animals to stop them fighting and killing each other, and generally to keep them quiet. I don't think I'd have kept that quiet if someone did that to me . . .

Be Kind to Wolves

The poor old wolf has always had a bad press (Little Red Riding Hood and all that), but brought up in a nice, homely environment, your average wolf *won't* bite your head off. He'll become a nice, well-behaved pet – given half a chance. So saying, it's fairly obvious that the first pets were more than likely to have been tame ex-wolves. It's also fairly clear that the

* Thank you, I think we get the point. Ed

offspring of these first pet wolves were also eaten and then worn by their masters on a regular basis.

Cattle

Your everyday, common-or-garden cow originally came from the wild ox (which in turn came from the mighty auroch – see page 58) which was originally tamed and domesticated by the Natufian tribe in Palestine.

Useless Fact No. 1023

You probably know this, but it's worth mentioning that all pets and farm animals are simply weedy versions of those in the wild: cats from lions and tigers, cows from buffalo and oxen, dogs from wolves, goldfish from sharks, budgies from eagles . . .*

---

* OK, we get the point, now you're getting silly. Ed

$\mathbb{G}$ *BEASTLY BEASTIES (STONE AGE WILDLIFE)*

Many of the animals that Stone Age man had to put up with were much nastier than the chaps we have today. Generally they were bigger and much crosser, which is no fun when all you've got to hunt them with are pointy sticks and bows and arrows (if you're lucky).

Here are some of the best – or the worst – depending on which end of the spear you're at.

Mammoth

Take one standard elephant, cover him with long, red woolly hair and give him little ears. Make him almost half as big again, shove a huge hump up at the neck end of his back and add massive sharp, curved tusks – and you have . . . a mammoth.

Mammoths reached England from France and trudged on to Ireland in the days when we were all joined up. More is known about the Siberian Mammoth (*Mammuthus primigenius**) because almost perfectly preserved specimens have been found in that ancient deep-freeze they call Siberia.

* I didn't know they were clever. Ed
I'll do the jokes, thank you! JF

Useless Fact No. 1025

Sled dogs have been known to have fed on mammoth-meat, preserved in the ice for 30,000 years. It obviously didn't display sell-by date stickers! Mind you, I suppose if you're a hungry husky, and you're stuck in the middle of a frozen ice flow, you might not be that choosy.

Sabre-Toothed Cat

There seems to be a bit of an argument as to whether these vicious creatures were actually lions or tigers, but I like the idea of them being tigers – so there!

Take one standard tiger, rub off his stripes (doesn't that make him a lion anyway?*), make him much bigger, give him enormous curved, knife-like upper canine teeth (20 cm at least), massive neck muscles to enable his head to be brought down with enormous force and a jaw that could open to almost 90° and you have . . . the sabre-tooth tiger.

Sabre-toothed tigers, the most deadly of all the later prehistoric animals, died out with the extinction of their favourite dinner, the mastodon (coming soon), which was

* No, stupid. Lions and tigers are different sub-families of Felidae. Ed
I only asked. JF

hunted out of existence by us lot. Unlike modern lions and tigers, the larger sabre-tooths were capable of killing mammoths and rhinos by simply slicing through their thick flesh and hanging on till the poor bleeders bled to death.

Useless Fact No. 1028
The best examples (dead of course) of the sabre-toothed whatever-they-were were found pretty well-preserved in the La Brea Tar Pits in Los Angeles (enough to kill anyone). Apparently the silly billies had chased their prey into the tar and then couldn't get out themselves (see Bad Hunting Methods in Ancient Times).

Cave Lions
This time, take a lion and *add* a few stripes. Make him at least a quarter bigger than your modern everyday lion (and twice as nasty), then ask him to hide in European caves over 10,000 years ago and jump out on your ancestors.

Woolly Rhinoceros
A bit cuter than the ones we have now (it's amazing what a bit of hair can do*), the woolly rhino lasted right up to the end of the last major ice age. It spent its life nibbling the tundra on the edges of the glaciers and shovelling snow with the huge flat horn on the end of its nose. Nobody seems to know what the smaller one behind it was for (maybe a bottle opener).

Auroch
If you want to find the great-great-great-great-great-great (etc., etc.) grandparents of the modern cow you need go no further than the auroch. Extinct from the 17th century, this wild ox was the guy you see in all the cave paintings, being chased

* How would you know, baldy? Ed

around by stroppy stick men. He was a big fellow, 3.5 metres long, 1.8 metres tall at the shoulder, black as a bin bag, with massive forward-pointing horns. Unlike his modern descendants, the auroch was a mean critter and extremely dangerous to hunt. He was often confused with the European bison (wrongly).

Cave Hyena

I always feel a bit sorry for hyenas. Nobody, but nobody (except perhaps their mums), loves 'em. They've got to be the nastiest, ugliest animals that have ever been.

EVEN I CAN'T LOVE THAT!

Like vultures, the hyena is a right parasite, seldom killing anything itself, but well happy to rush in as a gang and steal the food off those who've done all the hard work. Cave hyenas (so named because they presumably lived in caves) were even worse than the ones we get these days – they were bigger and meaner and spottier.

Cave Bear

Despite their terrible reputation, the massive cave bears were exclusively vegetarian, and rather nice – if you didn't try to kill them (sounds like me!). They'd spread all the way from North Africa to Europe but, despite being hunted nearly into extinction by Stone Age man, it's most probable that they died out completely from natural causes during the last big ice age.

Mastodon

A relative of our elephant, these guys lived from 1,600,000 years to 10,000 years ago and were spread evenly throughout the world. They were vegetarian leaf-eaters and were smaller and more stupid than our elephants, with littler ears, littler tusks, longer red hair and massiver legs.

Chapter 11

ONWARD AND UPWARD

It's a bit difficult to work out when man first picked up a lump of metal and thought it might just come in handy. Maybe he thought it was some kind of shiny stone, but then worked out that, however hard he hit it, bit it or threw it, it wouldn't shatter. At first copper was the only metal to be really useful. Gold, though pretty, was too soft (and he probably couldn't get much for it in those days). Man then realized that the yellower copper was tougher than the redder variety . . . He'd accidentally discovered the natural form of bronze, which he was later able to create by melting the copper down with other metals like tin or zinc.

Bronze, etc.

Bronze was the key to the whole future of the metal ages (bronze age, iron age) and, indeed, the key to *The Development of Mankind* (fanfare, please!). Bronze Age dates are not very exact, and the earliest date I can come up with is around 6500 BC years ago. Before then just about everything was made of pottery, stone or bone.

I TOLD YOU THAT YOU CAN'T HAVE A POTTERY HAMMER!

Bye Bye Stone

The discovery and use of metal probably began in Mesopotamia – it was here that the very earliest copper pendant (or copper *anything*, come to that) was found. From then on, I suppose, it's all just history because, give or take a couple of thousand years, we can safely claim that this discovery marked the beginning of the end of the Stone Age and, even more importantly, the beginning of the end of this book.

🐾 TIME'S UP

I hope this little book has gone some way to explain how your distant relatives (from the monkey side of the family) went about their daily business. More than that, I hope you found my version slightly less stuffy than the books that are usually served up on the subject. If you didn't, you haven't really wasted your money: you can always tear the pages out and make paper darts or something. Failing that, the paper's quite soft, so you might want to use it in the—*

If you're really into the Stone Age and all that business, why not try the local library for more information? Or you could start digging in your back garden. You never know, there might be some old mammoth bones under the lawn. Just don't tell anyone I suggested it!

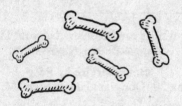

---

* Thank you, Mr Farman. I think we all get the message. Ed